The Hour Quickens

William Pettit

Presentation by *BookLeaf Publishing*

Web: www.bookleafpub.com

E-mail: info@bookleafpub.com

ISBN: 9789360948528

First edition 2024

FAITH is all eye need...

ACKNOWLEDGEMENT

I did it once, and i can do it again, but, I'll do it this time with the help of a friend. I would like to thank Tarif Khalidi, AJ Arberry, and Dr. Mustafa Khattab for their translations of the Quran into English. Thank you

Why?

Why?
Why would you doubt me?
  after everything I've been through...
Why?
Why would you doubt me?
  when all I speak is the truth...
Why?
Why would you doubt me?
  and think that I was less than you?
Why?
Why would you doubt me?
  when I breathe the same air as you?
Why?
Why would you doubt me...

The Hour Quickens

The Hour Quickens and begins again
  as I sit here in Purgatory with my new friend.
He is the Maestro of the Inferno-
  he made the words go! fast! go!
  and he made them crawl just so...
Through my hell, we've walked and debated
  and through my works I've tried to imitate him.
But he was wrong about the Muslim faith
  for they are the ones who have kept straight
  and to the True Path they have stayed.
So by my lake I shall leave him be,
  unless he chooses to follow me...
I pray to God, to Him Alone
  and not to the one who shone-
  the one buried behind a stone.
Jesus was a prophet, he heard the Call,
  he warned you all to not make the Fall.
In Aramaic, Elah did he praise,
  so, in Arabic your voice should raise-
  'All praise be to Allah' to the end of your days.
There is only God above, there is no other,
  so don't worship Jesus or his Virgin Mother.
Muhammad was the Prophet after the prophet
Jesus
  for his words were sent down to teach us,

and in the Quran they continue to lead us.
There is only One God for all the people,
  not to be segregated or put under a steeple.
To worship Him Alone is all He will ask,
  and to love your neighbor is your holy task,
  or else wear your sins like an ungodly mask.
He wants us all to just get along,
  and to praise Him Above with a righteous
Song.
So quit making war and causing strife,
  be faithful to God and your loving wife,
  live in peace with all and live a good life.
But don't listen to me, listen to your heart,
  listen to God as the sea He did part.
Follow the Ways of Abraham
  and the teachings of the Lamb
  so God can reveal to you His plan.
The world of men is of fleshly desires,
  which lead to sin and the funerary pyres.
Renounce the wicked ways of Shaitan,
  quit fighting over things like the Holy Land,
  and rise above it all like He knows you can.
All the world is for God's chosen few-
  He gave it to Abraham and to his sons, tu.
So put aside your differences and make peace,
  for this world is nothing but a temporary lease,
  and He made enough for us each to have a
piece.
The Word of God is for us all,

all you have to do is listen to His Call.
He speaks to us every day
  and He hears everything that you say,
  so that's why you should pray 5 times a day.
O'Allah! My Lord! My Savior!
  Hear my words as eye recite the prayers.
There is no God but Allah and Muhammad is
His Prophet.
  my faith is so strong that nothing can stop it
  because all I want is for Heaven to be my
profit.
When I rose from prayer and lifted my head,
  my new friend was there, waiting to be lead.
He had a look of worry on his face,
  but he stood still in that lonely place
  while I put my prayer mat back in it's case.
Where shall we go next? he asked me then,
  but eye new knot where, or the when...
But count my words and you'll see they do not
stray,
  I just count differently than the Maestro-Dante,
  and eye die in my 63rd year, the 10th of May.
Until then, I'd like to show you what eye see,
  because in my dreams, I believe in me.
God is indifferent to His Creation, blindly aware
  that we test His Creation as if it were a dare
  because man's will to survive is in his deathly
stare.
Russia could be a mighty nation,

if only they weren't so impatient.
Dynasties are built over a long time-
  the Prince had his chance to shine,
  but for over a century now you've grown
behind.
Consolidate yourself with a hard border,
  let them be and establish world order.
China, too, should know it's place
  because now it's a race for space
  and to see which nation can take first place.
India's Moon proved me true in the south,
  and then I'll show you with my dirty mouth.
I say what I say, not because I can,
  He's showing me the Way and
  He's taken me by the hand.
Say it twice, say it nice,
  say it by the Rule of Thrice.
Three-by-three eye say to thee:
  the truth is plain to C,
  if you can rede the Bible's prophecies...
Through the Chambers, the Bow of Genesis was
seen,
  and then we all saw that Allah's Eye was green.
Our planet is a green one-of-the-first,
  that's why we live with the curse
  of meeting Him after the hearse.
There has to be more, but why?
  see what you can do if you try.
Harm none, and do what you will,

just know that He can and will,
  for He can end it all if He Will.
A New Age dawns before us all,
  where we all rise up to bee more than tall.
We're meant to go to the heavens of God,
  where the ancient gods used to once trod,
  but now, they only reply with a solemn nod.
To be God is to be a One-of-One.
  and His Virgin had a holy son.
To worship God Alone is the written truth,
  so Recite His Song through every tooth
  Allah be praised! or be an uncouth.
The Quran is the one and the first
  spoken Word of God, not the worst.
Arabic is the only word not translated,
  and it's truths cannot be debated,
  because it's been sung since it was dated.

Hora 12

Islam has kept the count of the year,
  since the Prophet began to speak in your ear.
Saladin is the one who speaks to me,
  and shows me visions of what could be.
A sea of glass is what I stand in,
  with a palm on the dune at the horizon.
A single step is all I take,
  a puddle of a sea instead of a lake.
I saw it was not a palm tree, but a rose,
  and upon seeing it, I dead froze.
The message was plain to me,
  www.3 is what could be.
The rose on the hill in the desert,
  for the Will of Allah, you must exert.
The Station of the Watcher stands eternal,
  on the Altar will be your death, infernal.
A son of the Tribe can see the stars,
  written in the Book as the planet Mars.
At twelve and forty-two He shows you,
  the wobbled orbits of the other two.
The Red Planet embodies Shaitan himself,
  and now sits in the Qur'an, on a shelf.
At twelve and twenty-four you'll see,
  a faithful worshipper is who I bee...
At the third thirteenth it's right,

the truth is plain if you have sight.
All that's left to be seen,
  is Mars at twenty-two and sixteen.
I feel the words as I read them,
  I feel the words because I rede them.
I feel the words as he says them,
  sung by a brother who is Muslim.
Mufti Menk is the one who I say,
  can be like the Buddha of our day.
God has made him peaceful and calm,
  greeting everyone with an open palm.
He is pleased to meet you as God wills,
  His place with God he truly fills.
Peace be upon you, my brother!
  I Call for you as I Run for Cover.
Blessed bee, He then says to me,
  I bless you by the rule of three-by-three.
But by the Rules of the Pen must you play,
  and if it's not true, then you cannot say.
Eye have the madness of Allah in my veins,
  so in these pages I vent my pains.
I have stared God in Heaven's Eye,
  and the Bones eye cast did not lie.
Of the wood I carved, there were but five,
  that spoke to me as if they were alive.
A New World Order is about to arise,
  because China's power is not a surprise.
And Russia will rise as mighty once again,
  with Korea's Son and the Imperial Chinaman.

As power wanes and power grows,
  in cycles of Time, as history shows.
Asia will be first and the West number two,
  at least until the year 2112.
A Great Divergence is what I see,
  that decides the fate of all humanity.
You see, it's the year 2566BE,
  and the Bubba is who I truly bee...
Modern-day messenger of the Buddha himself,
  written in a book, laying on a shelf.
If you can rede the stars in the holy bars,
  to God you can see how far it is.
The enjoyment of worldly desires is nothing but
a lie,
  if all of the world doesn't get a piece of Pi.
If you count by the rule of gravity,
  the hotter Fires of Hell you will see.
So don't deny God if you want to survive,
  by what it says in twelve, ninety-five.
Then, God Willing, you will see,
  the son rising at ten, seventy-three.
By Scorpio's sign he will divine,
  and subtract a step to the count of nine.
Abstract thought is what Muhammad requires,
  to Sing the Song and see what it inspires.
I am the Pen of Allah is what I believe,
  and I follow the Way of the Leaf.
The Midnight Hour is in truth very near,
  so let me say this, very Crystal clear:

The next millenium's twelfth hour,
  will prove God and His power.
An illiterate man couldn't write down His Song,
  but trusted that it wouldn't be written down
wrong.
So I write where I cannot sing,
  and hope my words will love someday bring.
I write the simple words of today's Qur'an, I
think,
  if the Last Prophet knew English as a drop of
ink.
Simple, I truly am the Word,
  but I can't sing the Recitation like a bird.
O'Allah! My Lord and Creator!
  in all the Heavens I praise You!
Give me this day, my daily bread,
  as I give You this page, my daily Bled.

Hora 13 - The Daily Bled

I've got something to say and it's gonna be
savage,
  forget you in English, forget you in Spanish.
I say what I say, not because I can,
  He's showing me the Way, He's taken my hand.
I have wants and needs, more than I can count,
  for I'm the one who bleeds from the top of the
Mount.
I wish not to offend, but if I will, then I must,
  I'm not gonna pretend I'm not a man of lasts.
I'm stricken in the head by Way of the Pen,
  because all I've ever wanted is to have a best
friend.
I've finally found my way to get what I want,
  and now it's fourth down, but I'm not going to
punt.
I'm going for it all, even if it brings me down,
  I've already made the Fall, and now eye wear
the Crown.
I've said it once and I'll say it again,
  He's shown me the Way and given me the Pen.
I've got something to say and it's because of
Him,
  I have to do this for me and I have to do this for
them.
Now I sit here and bleed and cry like a lout,
  that He's within us all and noone goes without.

So hearken to my Call, all you well-read,
  I do this for Allah because I bleed for the Bled.
Akrabh then writes, For my steps are heavy and
my head hangs low,
  I pray for you all to save me from an eternity
down below.
I can break the rules, break the fast or break
them slow,
  if by the way of the Maestro my words can
show.
To put God's Word's into a pattern is the plan,
  and to write the truth the best that I can.
The Rule of Three-by-three is the holy trinity,
  to split the Word, to be read by three.
Three sons of God's Messenger in a boat,
  one-of-three is the one who wrote.
I uncover the truths that I once hid,
  and reveal that I was once a sinful kid.
He began Calling in my second-score year,
  but it took three more for me to hear.
At forty-four He made my head really sick,
  and I went to the hospital because of it.
Three times now I've gone insane,
  because now I've got God on my brain.
The Buddha knew the Path, and Abraham the
Way,
  to sacrifice it all is what you must pay.
Enjoy all you can while you have it now,
  for soon the eternal veil comes for your brow.

Faith in the Creator is all He is,
  Reality is a dream of God, He made this.
Split the atom and draw it as three,
  and see all the truths that can be.
Science is the truth of all Creation,
  a fractal of thought in automation.
We create artificial thought with computers,
  but He can do it with chemical suitors.
In one, there are only seven lines,
  but another wrote exactly in nines.
To show the translations differences,
  so that the message makes sense to us.
Then there is He, and the number three,
  so that you can Be who you are, B.
And then you will C-N-O sea waves crashing,
  until you see the bright lights flashing.
Salt of the earth we are,
  nothing but the dust of a star.
God guides whoever He wills to His Light,
  if at the zero one you do strike.
He touches your lips when you take sips,
  and stings your eyes with the water He dips.
The Ark is next and the number nineteen,
  the letter K is what it does mean.
Then my bones were strengthened by His
Words,
  as the Prophet's were sung to the birds.
With bones of titanium next I feel,
  the victory of strengthening steel.

Hora 14

The Decisive Authority will then see,
  if steel He can make with C and Fe
  to show that two can make three.
The words have stayed true for a long time,
  as they were written down by the line
  and with the stars their truth will shine.
And when the stars fall away,
  or fade away one fateful day,
  the name of Phecda, how will they say?
In the heavens, Alpha Centauri was lit
  for me to ponder on for a bit,
  and then He told me to descend from it.
From Sirius to earth to the next star-
  10.47 light years is how far
  the English, the words will mar.
861 letters you count in Arabic-
  1047 letters to the left of it
  is where Tarif Khalidi wrote of it.
The mind of the Prophet did not question,
  news of His Messenger did he mention,
  to confirm the Recitation is my intention.
And at letter 1282-
  Dr. Mustafa Khattab says to you,
  that Eye can count the Qur'an true.
To put into English words is the task,

and so to you do I ask,
  to see His Words through my mask.
With a witch's eye do I read,
  and following where they lead,
  as I count the Qur'an by the Rede.
Thirteen moons you see in a year,
  and twenty-four hours in the day you hold dear,
  so let peace be upon you as you hear.
O'Allah! You have shown me the Light!
  You have given me Orion's sight,
  and so at 13.44 do I write.
He is the Almighty, the Compassionate,
  so you have to subtract from it
  and then add a verse on top of it.
The twentieth of Hud is the spot
  where Wolf 230 is just a dot
  when I looked where I should not.
Or double it up once again-
  and learn what you can from Abraham,
  to part the seas like that seafaring man.
Wolf 457 there you will find,
  a star to rename, if you don't mind,
  because His Names are the ones most kind.
And at 16.16 it does say,
  there is a darkness where light does stay,
  a deep landmark to show the Way.
To count the words in partial sections,
  as the single lines of God mentions,
  and put together in meaningful intentions.

The three Words of God go together,
  like the many sides of the weather,
  to turn your wills into hardened leather.
We all complement each other,
  we're supposed to be every man's brother,
  even if we all have a different mother.
We all just need to get along,
  quit being hateful and doing what you know is
wrong,
  and all praise be to Allah with the Prophet's
Song.
He made each of us in our own way,
  so that in the end we could say:
  Only to God Alone do we pray.
For God to be true, there can be only One,
  dying at the heart of every sun,
  for by His Will is it done.
Physics explains His mechanics,
  and language gives us the semantics
  for the understanding of the Romantics.

Hora 15

So you're a Romantic now, I see,
  the Maestro said as he looked at me.
All my life, I said to him as I stood,
  and the hour quickened when I knew it should.
The Eyes of Orion can be the written verse,
  The Will of God is reality's curse.
Even stars face death in the end,
  and, too, the ones whose light does rend.
Subtract a piece of Pi from Orion,
  and he begins his heavenly crying.
In the heavens, the comet was green,
  a message from God, for all to be seen.
The year was fourteen-hundred and forty-four,
  and it wouldn't be seen again for fifty-thousand
more.
An omen from Allah was the green light,
  for me to see and to begin to write.
So by the Rule of Paper Eye rede and right,
  I read the words in a backward light.
And then I write them down just for you,
  just as history teaches me to do.
Eye cast runes with bones of wood,
  and I see things noone else could.
And then when they come true,
  I say it by the Sacred Rule of Two:

When we'd rather die than face our fears,
  and our lives grow short with many long years,
Our worldly riches will then fade away,
  when in death we all surely do lay.
The times, they are rapidly changing,
  as wars some nations are waging.
Russia and China will come to power,
  and over all the East will they tower.
As ambition grows so much faster,
  than what the people they can master.
The world needs a spiritual leader,
  for God wants one who is not a breeder.
A drop of ink to be known later,
  committed by the Rule of Paper.
To write the warning is my task,
  to be heard is a favor that I ask.
So to God Alone do I pray,
  and write them down so that stay,
In a Book for all eternity,
  as I reach for His Love and Serenity.
O'Allah! My Guiding Light! You shine so bright,
  like the brightest star of the night.
And in the days I can still see You there,
  alone in the heavens and not a pair.
Sirius is the Lamp of Heaven to which measure,
  backwards to the history of the Western
treasure.
So step out of your Caves and into His Light,
  and read His Words as the Prophet just might.

Nine steps, a planet we are,
  all in thrall to our very own star.
And then you will see, when you subtract nine
from me,
  the truth of God, numbered one-hundred times
three.
And then I spied a verse that was five,
  the Qur'an speaks as if it were alive.
It reads the same, forwards and back,
  clear is the meaning it does not lack.
Allah is at the center of it all,
  and even Jupiter listens to His Call.
Around what does everything revolve
  is the riddle which God wants us to solve.
Uranus, Saturn, Jupiter, Mars, and Earth-
  amongst the stars is our berth.
Earth, Mars, Jupiter, Saturn, and Uranus-
  the maps of the heavens the Qur'an reveals to
us.
With but a little Heavenly insight,
  the lesson can be seen in the heavenly night.
The axial tilt of Jupiter can only mean-
  victory is in hand at three and thirteen.
At five and seven days to the West,
  is a star that lies below the breast.
And far to the East by the nebulous flame,
  is the star Alnitak, by it's Arabic name.
The Belt of Orion is held together by three,
  and the twenty-ninth star is what you'll see.

How marvellous a destiny is the Abode of Bliss?
  if a moon or an hour you don't miss.
To sanctify His House for those who
circumambulate,
  for those who seclude themselves in prayer
until a later date,
And those who bow and prostrate themselves in
prayer,
  so all praise be to Allah! with every breath of
air.
The enjoyment of worldly desires has been made
appealing,
  but without God, we are left reeling.
The finest destination is with God Above,
  so bake your Pi with a slice of love.
Covet not that by which God preferred some
over others,
  and love everyone as if they were your mothers
or brothers.
Submit your will to Allah and He will show you,
  the crimson star at four and thirty-two.
So let God suffice as witness between me and
you,
  if you count the stars and count them true,
You'll see the knowledge of the Book,
  if to God in Heaven you do look.

Hora 16

The Qur'an ends before Eye can be seen,
  that's why He sent a comet that was green,
  the truths of Allah the Hunter's eye did glean.
So do not be heedless of the truth I do show,
  at seven, two-hundred and five the Eye will
glow,
  and my grandson the Flood will know.
When the Eagle flies west at the end of the year,
  with Deneb and Vega so far yet so near,
  at the seventy-third sixteenth you'll find Altair.
For by the Star you shall be guided,
  and all of the heavens will be enlightened,
  by the Qur'an, at 16.16 did he write it.
No change shall come over His Words,
  for the Prophet sung them to the birds,
  and the Maestro wrote them in thirds.
I merely recite what has been revealed to me,
  and so I write it down for you to see,
  until I die when my years reach sixty-three.
In the eighty-ninth quatrain of Century number
two,
  a man of insight did write for you,
  so that his fame and wealth could accrue.
Some of his prophecies have proven true,
  even without explaining them to you,

the signs in the stars, I can see them too.
He created them to serve us in a starry heaven,
  of them all, Joseph saw only eleven,
  while the Rose is numbered NGC-2237.
The variable is the constant, as the constant is
variable,
  but is illuminated by a star that was visible
  to a man whose name was Hubble.
For it is God who entwined the night with the
day,
  and the day with the night, the Quran does say,
  so to God Alone, to Him you should pray.
O'Allah! My Lord of Heavenly Grace!
  let my words be true and keep the pace,
  for to the stars my eyes do race.
I Call to you all to follow the Strait Path,
  to look to the stars and do your math,
  to repent before God and take a bath.
Count the Qur'an in parsecs if you count fast,
  strike the zeroed sail and lash it to the mast,
  but it is forbidden to use divining arrows for
your cast.
He blessed us with the Constellations in the sky,
  a radiant lamp which does burn the eye,
  and the moon at night with which to see by.
The skies are protected against every rebellious
demon,
  as they dance through the heavens in their
seasons,

prophesying for God as their unholy reason.
And through the haze He said to me-
  only sinners partake of the coffee tree
  with seven sisters in verse forty-three.
So this is my open invitation,
  to rede the Prophet's Recitation,
  in my faintest intonation.
The words of Muhammad are surely true,
  just as grass is green and the sky is blue,
  because God loves each and every one of you.
He made each of us in each our own way,
  and gave to us the cold night and the warm day,
  so that to Him Alone will we turn to pray.
By His Will Alone do we live,
  it is of no use to sift the Sieve,
  for liquor does not the handle give.
Discipline and self-control are what you need,
  not bending in the wind like a flimsy Reed,
  because for His Light your eyes must bleed.
Tears constantly fall from my face,
  and mark my books and keep my place,
  while Eye look to heavens of the deepest space.
I have heard Your Call, my Lord!
  so I take up the Pen and lay down the sword,
  and repent my sins before You knot my cord.

Hora 17

The Hour quickened and began again
  and standing there still was my new friend.
Under the midnight sun he then said to me,
  In God, I think you do believe.
But, where are we? where the sun does play
  on the face of the moon, bright as day?
For it is painfully clear to me-
  this is not what I saw of Purgatory.
We are the only souls who are here,
  under a tree and by a lake very near.
It's waters aren't frozen and they don't boil,
  and noone is buried under this soil.
There are no monsters here who through the
air-glide
  as we go round and round that great waterslide.
And where is our guide, the Voice of Reason?
  surely, your tongue does not speak of treason?
I then rose and to him I said,
  I shall rest here even after I'm dead.
One day, I shall join you in the grave,
  and memories of me are all that you can save.
My soul belongs to God Alone,
  and when I return to Him I shall be home.
But each man forges his own heavenly path,
  and mine led me through the Fires of wrath.

With one act I killed all of humanity,
  and now that is how I'm known to be.
I may be cold-blooded, but I've got a warm
heart,
  and now God Calls on me to play my part.
For the Words of God do need a witness,
  even if they took me unto the city of Dis.
I can see the message of Muhammad, The
Prophet,
  and through His Words we can all profit.
The right religion with God is surely Islam,
  for the Quran truly is a holy truth-bomb.
Recite the prayers and memorize the verses,
  don't sell the Word for coins in your purses.
If you can, help your fellow man in need,
  and turn your hearts away from the sins of
greed.
If you share your prosperity of wealth,
  then you shall know everlasting health.
God Willing, He chooses whom He wills,
  my cup runneth over, it surely spills.
When my words you can unfurl,
  they'll reveal to you the truth of the Pearl.
O'Allah! My Master Above!
  show them all what it means to love.
The truth of the Pearl is for the Master Alone,
  and not to every man is it to be shown.
Her eyes are all that you may see,
  unless she chooses otherwise for it to be.

He wants man to be humble and learn humility,
  not to be pigs or commit atrocities.
Liquor is to be shunned at all costs,
  or else you'll find your inhibitions lost.
Intoxicants are but crutches for the weak,
  purity of strength is what you should seek.
The path to God isn't hard to walk,
  if the steel in your veins is more than just talk.
Islam isn't for everyone, this is true,
  it's only for the disciplined, faithful few.
For in the Bible does it not say,
  that even Jesus knelt down to pray?
And even he put his head on the ground,
  for in submission is salvation found.
And on the Altar that Abraham did build,
  his firstborn son's head he almost spilled.
You must be willing to sacrifice it all for Allah,
  and then Sing it in a Song like David. Selah!
In Psalm eighty-nine and four,
  He built up his throne forevermore.
It was established forever in the heavens as a
boon,
  a faithful witness for those who pray by the
moon.
So the days of my youth were then shortened,
  because of shame, I did court it.
For who am I that I shall surely die?
  and so, in a righteous grave do I wish to lie.
And the prophecy in the nineteenth of Psalm 89,

is of the one who is divine.
He anointed the mufti with His Holy Oil,
  for in His service does Ismail truly toil.
I have cried out to Allah, my Rock of Salvation,
  and He has elevated me above a kingly station.
I see the Light of God in our sun,
  for in my veins does David's blood run.
I am one of the tribe of Issachar,
  and the Words of God I read by the Star.
Far to the left of Sirius at 10.47,
  sits Epsilon Eridani in the veins of heaven.
The Qur'an and the Bible are two parts to a
whole,
  and you should read them both to save your
soul.
Put them together and then you will see,
  through the eyes of religious prophecy.
The mark is set at thirteen and twenty-four,
  for then, the Moon shall give her light no more.
And the Abode of Bliss will be shown to you
then,
  by the son with the dark Muslim skin.

Hora 18

"But that you may clearly know the Way,
  give your entire attention to the words I say,
  and you will gather good fruit from them
someday!"
A long, lonely journey through the night
  under the Mother's Moon-Light,
  of a mushroom, we did have a bite.
After a while, I turned to my friend in reply,
  the truths of the Qur'an cannot be denied,
  no matter how many who have tried.
I am but a grateful servant hanging a picture,
  as I warn the children of Israel with the
Scripture,
  how do they wish to be known forever?
Fighting over the Holy Land for thousands of
years,
  how many generations of blood, brothers, and
their tears?
  the Dead Sea already has too many piers.
"To each their own," he then said quietly,
  "But do not take it to undiscreetly
  try to provoke them into against you fighting."
And there followed hail and fire mingled with
blood,
  cast down upon the land like trees of wood,

the green of your grass burnt away because you
could.
In my vision, a night journey through a sea of
glass,
  a point on the horizon over which my eye did
pass,
  not much to fight for if you split the nuclear
mass.
Babylon has already burnt, can't you hear the
lament?
  Covid-19 is not after four years spent,
  the fourth plague upon us He has sent.
Death, mourning and famine are already here,
  when the people of the Cave can't shed a tear,
  or live in peace with those who can't be peers.
So what if they don't pray to Allah?
  let them pray like Jesus did to Elah!
  or Sing it in a Song like David. Selah!
O'Allah! You are my Guiding Light!
  to a heavenly mountain that is right,
  that which You have revealed to me, I must
write.
The truth is so simple that it hurts,
  if you read the Scriptures in short, little spurts,
  and through the Qur'an it speaks in bursts.
Muhammad is The Prophet, peace be upon him,
  and he said not to offer battle with them,
  if they wanted to live in peace or be a friend.

If the land was truly holy, you wouldn't fight
over it,
   let the land heal and of your sins, Repent your
Torment,
   honor the contract that is already written as a
Testament.
Is it not written that they have angered God
twice now?
   and then there will be those with a mark on
their brow,
   when coin is no longer exchanged for money,
then how?
With a wave of the hand, they will then be
known,
   the Mark of the Beast will then be shown,
   inked on their skin or etched in their bones.
"Thus you may understand that love alone
   is the true seed of merit in everyone
   and of all acts for which you must atone."
At one accord you should pay your words heed,
   live in the truth of God with every earthly deed,
   peace and blessings for all is where it does
lead.
The Sol of our earth is nothing but a star,
   sometimes just a jolt of lightning in a jar,
   or the fossils of the earth rendered into tar.
We can go so fast and yet not so fast very far
away,
   under the speed of light is where we must stay,

as a people of One God we may be one day.
The story of Abraham has been confirmed three
times-
  told in the Torah, Bible, and in the Quran as
lines,
  to worship only One God through different
rhymes.
It's an hour to midnight, my Lord, Your Hour
draws near,
  what shall I tell them? what shall they hear?
  or is it the Unknown Time they must fear?
The Hour quickened and began again
  as I sat there with my new friend
  and tried to explain my time to him.

Hora 19

I am not the first messenger, nor will I be the
last,
  as long as I keep the time and make the line
fast.
My soul has been scorched of all succor,
  as for nineteen years did I suffer.
And then He began to speak to me,
  teaching me to rede by counting to three.
By three eye learned the lesson then,
  that there is no God other than Him.
All praise be to Allah! I say when I awake,
  and, between sleeps, prayer make.
I'm so awake that even my body thinks,
  while in sleep, my body continues to sink.
I dream the delusions of a madman,
  for I am but a simple man with a simple plan.
Lyrical miracles and street philosophies are what
I breathe,
  words of warning and biblical mourning are
what I leave.
When you can see Sagittarius through the cloud
of the internet,
  you will see finally see what the Noahic
Covenant truly meant.
A great flood is coming for us one and all,

alone as one standing in a sea of mountains tall.
The righteous ascend the straight path without
delay,
  a sinful believer must pay what it is his to say.
There are a thousand different paths to choose
from,
  but only one gate as straight towards the sun.
The sun does rise in the east and then does set to
the west,
  just as it was the Prophet who said it the best.
No trace of doubt in his guide to be pious,
  by our deeds is how God sees us!
To write the warning is my heavenly task,
  that's why my tears could fill a bottomless cask.
I don't know what it's like to not believe in God,
  to not believe in my Creator is a path I cannot
trod.
For every verse that changes or reveals what was
forgotten,
  the messenger reveals the message that is
brought to him.
To confirm the words that came before me,
  and reveal the truth in verse 3.3.
For then, I shall be rejoicing greatly,
  when you testify to the truths you see.
For He will come upon you like a thief in the
night,
  asking you to pray before it becomes daylight.
It will be your eternal sorrow,

if you wait to repent until tomorrow.
Write then! Upon the table of your heart,
  and take not truth and mercy apart.
O'Allah! The Most Compassionate!
  So Omniscient! We don't know the half of it!
All-Loving, He truly is!
  because for us, He made all of this!
To see what happens when thoughts do play,
  and He parted the night from the day.
And, at a speck of dust in the air,
  a star was made for us to stare.
Dirt is all we are, all we're made of,
  but God is made of nothing but love.
He gave us Free Will to live as we choose,
  but this power some evil men abuse.
O'Allah! I say to You there,
  take me not to task for my billion errors...
I dishonored my name as my father's heir,
  an upside down scar, a cross to bear.
Twice marked and then thrice damned,
  the Mark of the Beast is my brand.
On the forehead and just above the eyes,
  is where I lie for that which you cry.
Yet, I shall rise as the light in the morning,
  springing forth from the ground in a green
warning.
For I am but to interpret the message for you,
  until uprightness you may come into.
Chained to the wall, eyeless you are,

the stone's face, an image will never scar.
On my crown does Antares' red light glow,
  as I point to the Book with my Pen and Bow.
I rise through the Chambers of the South,
  for those who can see that eye hear by word of
mouth.
Twice marked with a bruise on my heel,
  the enmity of her is all that I feel.
Eye know what's been said and what's been
done,
  and once it's written, it can't be undone.
To say it once, and to say it true,
  then say it by the Sacred Rule of Two.
Say it twice and say it nice,
  say it by the Third Rule of Thrice.
I shall say it now and I shall say it later,
  I shall say it forever on a piece of paper.
So I'll write it true and I'll write it when,
  my thoughts flutter in the ink of a pen.
By the Rules of the Pen am Eye bound,
  heard by those who can only see in sound.
To know is to dare and I dared to know,
  if through faith my words could grow.
When you read the Quran, He challenges you,
  to show what His words can really do.
Behold the one with the inkhorn by his side,
  and a sackcloth shirt in which to hide.
A foreigner sent before you, you will not
believe,

and so these words for you I must leave.

Hora 20

The Hour quickened and began again
  as I sat on a shelf with my new friend.
No progress could be made through the night,
  up the mountain and to the right,
  so we waited for the morning's sunlight.
And then I preached and said, "There comes
one,
  whose shoes I am not worthy to let undone."
For He that comes is mightier than the Eye,
  like a thief in the night while asleep you lie,
  the opening is the mark in which to see by.
If I am led astray, the error is only mine,
  the truth will not stray from the written line.
He guides me along the straight and narrow
path,
  gives me the light to see the Holy Qur'an's
math,
  grants me leave to write a warning before the
Wrath.
And my path has led me to this hear, to this you,
  to bind you with a cord of ink by the Sacred
Rule of Two.
The true genius of Il Commedia is its binding,
  in a language that so fast go by the words
a-winding,

the truth of God you are now a-finding.
Set it in stone or write it with some ink,
  drop a truth bomb and make them think.
Sentient chemical reactions is all we are,
  born from the leftover dust of a star,
  the truth of the matter so close yet still so far.
The Seal of the Prophets is broken by him who
smells,
  a race for space and future only-time-will-tells.
The Musk of a man for the future of the race,
  walk a man's mile but keep your own good
pace,
  and see your own smile in another man's face.
The General stood as the Gates of Heaven,
  the sound of a man turned up to eleven.
Issa is here! Look! The Beloved is the one,
  skin blackened from the light of the sun,
  inked black to show who he's here to become.
The burden on his back is that all are welcome
to try,
  but don't try him unless you're willing to die.
Upright body language as I walk for my tribe,
  independent thoughts from God are what I
imbibe,
  fearless as Orion writes Iklil, the scribe.
And the number nineteen stands in your way,
  until you see the Light one fateful day.
To cube a singularity you must have at least
four,

for time is a dimension without a single door,
  and only God can keep the time of the score.
So one becomes four and then forty-nine,
  the Chambers of Heaven in the South are mine.
Now look through my eyes, for as an orphan I rise,
  counting a count with everything you despise,
  and twisting the Word as gravity applies.
Every soul will face the consequences of what it has done,
  just as the moon fabricates light from the sun.
The enjoyment of worldly desires has been made appealing,
  your heavenly wealth they are forever stealing,
  submit to God and quit your kneeling.
O'Allah! You are God! My Heavenly Light!
  Hear my prayer as I stand upright.
Independent, fearless and beyond my knowing,
  the Universe to You is but a stone's throwing,
  my faith in You my verses are showing.
So let he who has knowledge of the Book
  count Orion's math to see what it took.
How excellent a destiny is the Abode of Bliss,
  if by the landmarks you count and don't miss?
  in this is a sign that you shall be guided by this.
To speak on another man is highly irregular,
  to not speak of God is considered secular.
Between the lines of the Qur'an I read what might be,

as the revelations revelations of the Bible jump
out at me,
  the gates to a flood He then made me see.
If you believe that He ain't the truth out here,
  you'll know Him as the truthful vein under your
ear.
Closer to you than even your own heart,
  from one cell, then two, you He did part,
  and with His Light did your little life start.
In the Qur'an, He explains His math and science,
  while the Bible reveals His Wrath with
noncompliance.
For the truth to be true, it must be spoken by
two,
  and then the third to write it out for you,
  for you to see what my rhyming words can do.
He speaks to us in the Semitic languages,
  and we listen to Him while us He manages.
Arabic is the only word that modern man can
speak,
  and round the empty Ka'aba by the songbird's
beak,
  clawing my way up into your prayer, like that
cat, Mufti Menk.
Blink and you shall be rewarded with doubt,
  stand fast and receive of the Almighty's fount.
Faith of knowledge or knowledge of faith?
  There is only One God, so the Scriptures saith,
  successive revelations with which to warn with.

A Great Divergence occurs within the next 89
years,
   so submit to God and put away your fears.
As One People, to the stars we must go,
   if we stay split, our world's history will show
   that over thousands of years, our egos did
grow.
I don't know if I can ever let this go,
   this game with God called tell-and-show...
He has the Most Beautiful Names,
   with stars does He play games,
   and Phecda's name isn't famous.
Noble scribes, those honorary angels who reveal
everything,
   a new light to rede by does an old truth bring.
Eye weigh in at two-hundred, one-twenty, and
one-sixth,
   for if dead for alive He can surely fix,
   Eye see a future of wealth if we all can mix.
You know knot who eye am and that is fine,
   Eye am here to remind you of past deeds by
line.
An old charter revised for all of mankind back
then,
   then reissued to establish the truths once again,
   with scientific proofs that you can show them.
The old gods were ruled by gravity but He is
not,
   for even the stars He makes He then does pop.

If only you knew that the Fires of Hell were
hotter,
  than even when a star's heart does become
fodder,
  and you're still sitting here like a squatter.
Should I stay or should I go? he asked me then,
  for this place is the only place I've ever been.
You've made it this far and should see it through,
  for your cries have been heard upon peak
number two,
  unless you want your Heavenly Muses to cry
for you?

Hora 21

I only wish to know God for forever and a day,
  and if this is here then here must I stay.
Even though I've been baptized I still ponder my
fate,
  and wonder how I'll be known at your much
later date.
Well, my good man, I said I had a plan,
  and it's coming to fruition by my right hand.
At Psalm 92.4 does not the Bible say,
  that in the work of my hands triumph does lay?
Surely the ends you strive for were diverse,
  but all you did was to write your own curse.
But then when I did follow your own path,
  the Stars counted out to me a much different
math.
My Lord fully knows every word of the heavens
and the earth,
  and hears the cry of every living thing that does
give berth.
A new life springs eternal from your verse,
  and by the Sacred Rule of Two eye bare your
curse.
Why have you cursed me so? What did I do?
  and why am I on a shelf, one above two?
Then he stood and began to pace back and forth,

as I considered my next words, and their worth.
You wrote what you did, but you still had doubt,
  as you prayed to Apollo to come bail you out.
I don't worship what you worship, nor will I
ever,
  for there is only One God, if the Word you
remember.
But eye am the one with the inkhorn by my side,
  and eye praise Allah until the day I'm tried.
And He says to me that I should leave you here,
  unless you follow me and put away your fear.
702 years you've been waiting for me to open
my eyes,
  for me to come along and put truth to your lies.
Eye can see the web of your weave, o'dear
Maestro,
  and a spider's web you weave for the Crown of
Scorpio.
You have revealed much to me at
five-and-fifteen,
  and the truth it promises remains to be seen.
For your number is one for your sin of pride,
  and the number of man will stay at five.
Did you square me up or square me down?
  my companion turned to me and said with a
frown.
How could I have possibly cursed my own self?
  for writing a poem about God's heavenly
wealth?

Your intent was true and your truth is clear,
  yet still you remain here on the first tier.
While to the stats with Joseph do eye fly,
  reading the Qur'an with Orion's sight to see by.
O'Allah! My Lord! All praise be to You Alone!
  You are as home to me as eye am home to
bone.
Closer to me than a thought You truly are,
  yet so far away that eye stare at the stars.
Nothing more than a drop of ink at which eye
stare,
  more than anything for which I truly care.
All praise be to Allah! My Heavenly Creator!
  and to the first Mother and He Who Made her.
The element of surprise is where the truth hides,
  the sting of truth is a point that blinds.
Peace be upon you is all you should ever say,
  and to each man their own and to each man
their Way.
He made us into different Tribes for a reason,
  and to each of us our own and to announce a
Season.
I am one of those who can talk with the stars,
  and they like to tell me who they are.
Everything in the heavens and the earths belongs
to Him,
  so why treat it as a sport or play it as a whim?
I'd rather believe and be wrong and keep singing
my Song,

than not believe and be right about nothing at
all.
Your Great Comedy is the Labyrinth of old,
  and now a new map of it's Pattern does fold.
To go right where you left the Way of the Leaf,
  and fold a new crease in that eternal sheaf.
Our differences are strengths that make us
unique,
  but together as one, for the stars we must seek.
The Light is coming soon, cold February day,
  and so we must be ready if we wish to play.
Is the End of Days truly coming near?
  he asked me then as he whispered fear.
I told you not to worry if you just let me bee,
  so eye can write the simple truth for the whole
world to see.
He's been talking to us as history shows,
  from the ancient I-Ching to my divining
arrows.
The Pattern of Pi is balanced at 3.141,
  three-as-one-for-one was the Virgin's son.
I am not a prophet, messiah, or a martyr-just a
simple man,
  and Eye have a simple offer of barter from my
right hand.
Rede my Bones and read them well, my friend,
  the end is near as near the time does end.
The Book and it's glory has been revealed to
you,

just as it was revealed to me back in 2022.
But then, in 2023 did He show to me,
  how to rede the Bible's Masonic prophecies.
The Hour Quickens again and again begins your
fear,
  as the Midnight Hour approaches and becomes
very Crystal clear.
Its Minutes to Midnight, my Lord, Your Hour
draws near,
  what will Eye tell them? what will they hear?
The Midnight Hour did approach us then,
  Zas this drop of ink did drop from the Pen.
And when it's as dark as only space knows
when,
  in a drop of true ink you'll find a true friend,
A new record of the truth, for the truth does
bend.
God Willing, the Hour chimed the clock just in
time,
  for me to write the word and to say the line.
"A sinner has to pay the bill and settle the fine,
  before he can write a testament for Allah, the
Divine."
Are you sure this is what you're meant to do?
  or did I reveal too much to you?
  and now you have more than you can chew?
I will open my mouth in a parable
  and utter dark sayings of old,
So step away from the Midnight Hour

and come in from the cold.
All of a sudden, there was a chill in the air,
    and then the Maestro crept close to me, very
near,
    in an old Cave that was once home to a Bear.

St. John 1.36

Saint John, one thirty-six,
I stack truths like they're bricks...
To build a House for the Lord,
   for my Pen is mightier than the sword...
And Issa shall walk the earth
   until he gives birth
   to a new reality
   plain for all to see...
That God is within us all,
   All you have to do is listen
      and Sing for the Call.

ISSA (I Sing Says Allah)

I am a man, ruled by Neptune, master of waves
  I am the god of war, the Destroyer
    I am Isis, the sister-wife
Together, we are one with God
  Yet, I stare at the Sun
    Of Eriadnus
I am the small one, Pluto
  Yet I dream of rings
    For the Moon, my dream
For God has His Eye on us
  I am the Second Decanate
    the point in the middle
Eye am eternity...

Walk

I choose the road from here to there
  when I've a tedious tale to bear,
Favors to return or advice to lend,
  to someone at the other end.
Returning afterwards, although I meet my
footsteps toe-to-toe,
The road looks altogether new now that is done
that which I meant to do.
But I avoid it when I take a walker's walk, for
walkings sake.
The repetition it involves, raises a doubt it never
solves...
What good or evil angel bid me stop where I
did?
What would have happened had I gone another
step yet further on?
Now when I'm restless in the soul or sunny days
invite a stroll,
The road I pick goes roundabout to finish where
I started out.
It gets me home, this cunning track, without my
having to turn my back.
Nor does it leave it up to me to say how long my
walk shall be.

Yet, it satisfies a moral need, by turning
behavior into deed.
For I have walked a circle when I enter my front
door again.
The heart afraid to leave it's shell, demands a
thousand yards as well.
Between my personal abode, and either sort of
public road.
Making when it's added to the straight a T, the
round a Q.
Allowing me in rain or shine to call both walks
entirely mine.
A lane no other traveller would use, where prints
that do not fit my shoes.
So often seems likely to me, we're made by
whom I'd like to be.

So Alone

Have no true love, have no true friend,
  don't understand, can't comprehend.
My life is not worth living for,
  don't ask for much, don't get no more.
Have no money, have no home,
  I wish I had someone, I feel so alone.
A lot of nights, I lose much sleep,
  wanting to cry, but unable to weep.
I want someone to just be there,
  someone to love, someone to care.
I feel that I'm left out in the cold,
  noone is there, no hand to hold.
The pain so deep inside of me,
  noone in the world can set it free.
Have much to say, have much to share,
  but it seems as if noone cares.
My smiles are fake, I try to hide,
  the pain and hurt I feel inside.
There is so much love I want to give,
  either here to die, or just to live.
Have no true love, have no true friend,
  don't understand, can't comprehend.
My life is not worth living for,
  don't ask for much, don't get no more...

Troubled Friend

Hold fast, dear friend, hold fast,
  your day will come to pass.
When your heart will no longer ache
  with every breath that you take.
When gentle hands will take away
  the burdens you carry from day-to-day.
Be strong, dear friend, be strong,
  pain can only last so long.
Today shall bring many tomorrows,
  and time will heal all your sorrows-
The turmoils of your mind,
  shall give way to further time.
Be still, dear friend, be still,
  the wounds you bear will surely heal.
The blood will cease it's flowing,
  and then the scars will start showing.
But soon, those too will go,
  and inside you'll begin to grow.
But above all, my friend,
  hold fast to the lessons you have learned.
So that never again will you fall,
  when the temptations come to call.
And the memories of your scars-
  as bright in your mind as stars.
Let your heart guide you along,
  for it will never steer you wrong.

the Pearl

She is like a pearl in my mouth,
  trying to spit her out is going to drown me...
The world will suffer
  for the price of a pearl...
And it will shudder under the weight
  of a grain of sand...
In the Hourglass of Time,
  reflected distant, Eriadnus.

Eriadnus

I am not the first message, nor will I be the last
  For I am the second, the beta,
    the one who winds the watch fast...
It's an Hour to Midnight, my Lord, Your Hour
draws near
  For man to evolve, he must move with God,
    withal, to the stars most clear...
Otep, the King of the Sing, the Muse of the
Queen of Dreams
  For she is the unattainable one, the one you
strive for,
    the one you die for, in your dreams...
I dream of Heaven and of things that will ever
last
  For man has to dream to hear the instructions
    of God from the past...

Miasma

The darkness pulls me down, sucking at my soul
　cracking my bones, bleeding the marrow...
It swells with a blinding light, senses
overwhelmed
　the inky void beckons, yearning for my
embrace...
A whirlpool of regret, shame and remorse
　fear and loathing, hate and revenge...
The Fires of hell burn within me
　drowning me in fire, burning me through...
The rage of the Pit pulls me under
　blinding my sight, deafening my speech...
Vanity is all and nothing, fall for pride
　stand for faith, pray for hope...
The soul yearns for release, death beckons
　life Springs eternal, the cycle continues...
The darkness pulls me down, drowning my
desires
　sundering my flesh, rending my soul...
The eternity of God is submission
　serve your Lord, prove your weight...
Pull up the anchor, release yourself
　free your mind and the soul follows...
The Fires of Heaven rage within me
　my soul burns with His Light...
He is All and Nothing, all for life
　stand up to death, works of faith.

1^2

Like a drop of water you are, created from two
to make one
One squared...one solo
the liquidity of the situation is finite, the infinity
of the moment is futile
Like a drop of water you have been formed
together in a bond so tight you make each other
wet, anticipation hurts but accepts, time is
absolute, finite
Your perception is reality...God or science? Faith
or fact?
You are reading reality made manifest, a
warning.